WITHDRAWN

A Pet's Life

Cats

Anita Ganeri

Heinemann Library
Chicago, Illinois

www.heinemannraintree.com
Visit our website to find out
more information about
Heinemann-Raintree books.

To order:

☎ Phone 888-454-2279

🖳 Visit www.heinemannraintree.com
to browse our catalog and order online.

© 2009 Heinemann Library
an imprint of Capstone Global Library, LLC
Chicago, Illinois

Customer Service: 888-454-2279

Visit our website at www.heinemannraintree.com

Printed and bound by South China Printing Company Ltd

13 12 11 10 09
10 9 8 7 6 5 4 3 2 1

Library of Congress Cataloging-in-Publication Data
New edition ISBN: 978 14329 3389 0 (hardcover) – 978
14329 3396 8 (paperback)
The Library of Congress has cataloged the first edition as
follows:
Ganeri, Anita, 1961-
   Cats / Anita Ganeri.
      v. cm. -- (A pet's life) (Heinemann first library)
Includes bibliographical references and index.
Contents: What is a cat? -- Cat babies -- Your pet cat --
Choosing a cat
-- Things to get ready -- Welcome home -- Feeding time --
Training your
cat -- Playing with your cat -- Growing up -- A healthy cat
-- Old age.
   ISBN 1-4034-3993-1 (Hardback) -- ISBN 1-4034-4269-X
(pbk.)
   1. Cats--Juvenile literature. [1. Cats. 2. Pets.] I. Title. II.
Series.
   SF445.7.G36 2003
   636.8--dc21
                              2002151591

Acknowledgments
The author and publishers are grateful to the following for
permission to reproduce copyright material:
Alamy pp. **15** (© Juniors Bildarchiv), **16** (© isobel flynn); Ardea pp.
4, **18**, **19** (John Daniels); © Capstone Global Library Ltd. pp. **12**, **25**
(Tudor Photography); Corbis p. **27** (© David Shopper), **17**; Dorling
Kindersley pp. **10** (Daniel Pangbourne), **14** (Jane Burton); Getty
Images p. **21** (Steve Lyne); NaturePL.com p. **24** (© Jane Burton);
RSPCA pp. **8** (Andrew Forsyth), **23**, **26** (Angela Hampton); Warren
Photographic pp. **5**, **6**, **7**, **9**, **11**, **13**, **20**, **22** (Jane Burton).

Cover photograph of a tabby cat reproduced with permission of
Shutterstock (© mares).

The publishers would like to thank Judy Tuma for her
invaluable assistance in the preparation of this book.

Every effort has been made to contact copyright holders of
any material reproduced in this book. Any omissions will
be rectified in subsequent printings if notice is given to the
publisher.

Contents

What Do Cats Look Like? 4
Cat Babies. 6
Choosing Your Cat 8
Things to Get Ready 10
Welcome Home 12
Feeding Time. 14
Training Your Cat. 16
Playing With Your Cat 18
Growing Up. 20
A Healthy Cat 22
Your Pet Cat. 24
Old Age 26
Useful Tips. 28
Fact File 29
Glossary. 30
More Books to Read 31
Index 32

Some words are shown in bold, **like this**. You can find out what they mean by looking in the Glossary.

What Do Cats Look Like?

There are many kinds of pet cats. Cats can be big or small. They can have long, fluffy fur, or short fur. Cats are very popular pets.

This cat has long, fluffy fur.

This picture shows the different parts of a cat's body. You can see what each part is used for.

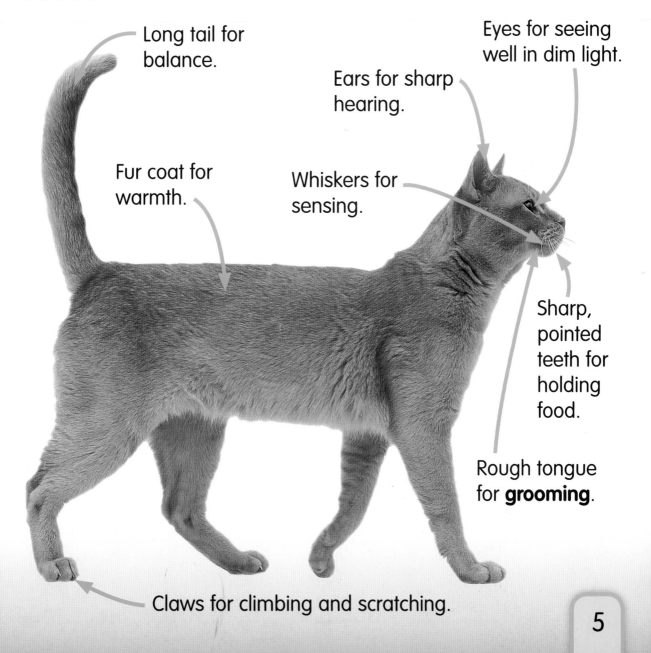

Long tail for balance.

Eyes for seeing well in dim light.

Ears for sharp hearing.

Fur coat for warmth.

Whiskers for sensing.

Sharp, pointed teeth for holding food.

Rough tongue for **grooming**.

Claws for climbing and scratching.

Cat Babies

Baby cats are called kittens. A newborn kitten is small and helpless. Its mother **grooms** it to keep it clean. The kitten opens its eyes when it is five to ten days old.

Newborn kittens feed on their mother's milk.

Kittens love to play with their brothers and sisters.

Kittens must be eight to ten weeks old before they can leave their mother. Then they are ready to be chosen as pets.

Choosing Your Cat

The best place to find a cat or kitten is an **animal shelter**. They are always looking for good homes for cats of all kinds and ages.

Adult cats often need good homes, too.

Choose a cat or kitten with bright eyes, a clean nose, and fur that is clean and shiny. Check that its bottom is dry and clean. Be sure it does not have fleas.

Things to Get Ready

Get everything ready before you bring your new pet home. Your cat will need a cozy basket or bed to sleep in. It will need bowls for food and water.

Put your cat's bed in a clean, quiet place.

Clean the litter box every day. Always wash your hands afterwards.

Your cat will need a plastic **litter box** where it can go to the bathroom. You can buy one from a pet store.

Welcome Home

You can carry your cat home in a special pet carrier made from plastic with a wire door. Put a small blanket or towel at the bottom of the carrier.

A pet carrier is also useful for taking your cat to the **veterinarian**.

If you have another cat or dog, let your new cat get to know it slowly.

For a few days, keep your new pet in one room to help it get used to its new home. Then you can let it explore the whole house.

Feeding Time

You can feed your cat dry or canned food. Adult cats need two meals a day. Kittens should have three to four smaller meals.

Kittens should eat special kitten food until they are one year old.

Wash your cat''s food and water bowls every day.

Make sure that your cat always has fresh, clean water to drink. It is not a good idea to give your cat or kitten milk. Milk might make your pet sick.

Training Your Cat

Kittens have to be trained to use a **litter box**. Start by lifting your kitten gently into its box. Do this often until it learns to use the box by itself.

Your kitten will soon learn to use the litter box on its own.

Cats that live indoors stay healthy. They do not often get hurt.

Keep your cat indoors where it has food, water, a bed, toys, and its litter box. Cats that live indoors are healthier and safer. They will live longer, too.

Playing With Your Cat

Cats and kittens love to play. You can buy special cat toys from the pet store. Cardboard tubes, rubber balls, and paper bags are also good toys for your pet.

Playing will teach your kitten new skills.

Your cat has to scratch with its claws to keep them sharp. The best place for your cat to scratch is a tall scratching post.

A cat's scratching post is covered with carpet or rope.

Growing Up

Kittens grow up very quickly. By the time they are one year old, they are adult cats. Older cats should be given senior cat food to eat.

Adult cats can be many sizes, from quite small to large.

As it gets older, your cat will still like to play.

Cats that are well cared for and that are kept inside live longer, healthier lives. If you get a new adult cat, take it to the **veterinarian** for a checkup.

A Healthy Cat

You need to look after your cat to make sure that it stays healthy. If you are worried about your cat, take it to a **veterinarian**.

If your cat stops eating or drinking, it may be sick.

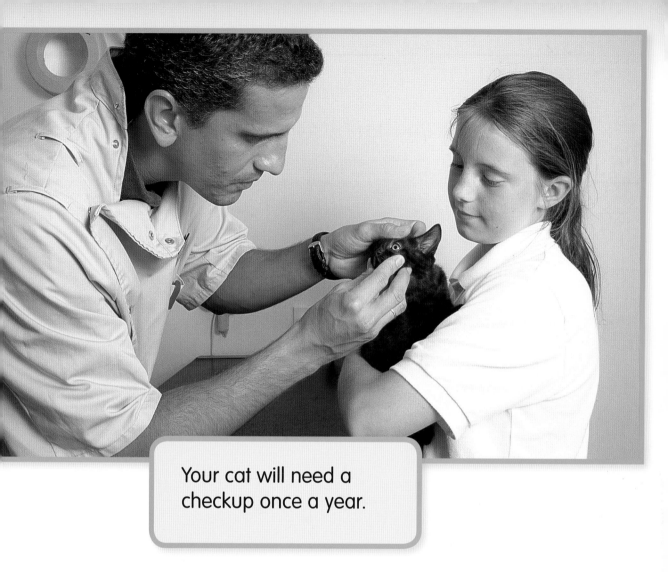

Your cat will need a
checkup once a year.

The veterinarian will give your cat shots to
stop it catching **diseases**. If you want to stop
your cat from having babies, the vet will
arrange for it to be **spayed** or **neutered**.

Your Pet Cat

Looking after a cat is fun, but it also takes lots of time. You need to look after your cat every day, for its whole life.

If you take good care of your cat, it will quickly become your best friend.

If you go on vacation, ask a friend or neighbor to look after your cat. It is important to leave the phone number of your cat's **veterinarian**, too.

Be sure to leave a list of what your friend needs to do for your cat while you are away.

Old Age

Cats can live for a long time, usually for about 12 to 16 years. As your cat gets older, it might need special care.

A senior cat will want to sleep more.

Older cats cannot see or hear as well as young cats. Jumping becomes hard, too. But your cat will still like to be held and cuddled.

Caring for your cat will help you learn how to treat animals properly.

Useful Tips

- The **vet** can fit your cat with a **microchip** so that it can be easily found if it gets lost. Otherwise, your cat should wear a **collar** and tag that has your name and address on it. Choose a quick-release collar that will come off if it gets caught on something.

- Cats like to be clean. They **groom** themselves with their rough tongues. Long-haired cats need to be brushed every day. This will stop them from swallowing too much fur and getting **fur balls**. It will also stop their fur from getting messed up and matted.

- Ask your **veterinarian** what you should do to stop your cat from getting fleas and worms.

- Look at the label on the cat food to find out how much to give to your cat. Do not give your cat too much to eat.

Fact File

- Cats were first kept as pets about 4,000 years ago. They were used to catch mice and rats.

- Cats were popular pets in ancient Egypt. People thought they were gods who could do magic.

- Cats can sleep for 16 to 18 hours a day.

- The oldest pet cat known was called Crème Puff. It live to be 38 years old. It died in 2005.

- Your pet cat's wild relatives include lions, tigers, leopards, and cheetahs.

- Most cats have 18 toes, five on each front paw and four on each back paw. Cats with 20 or more toes are called "polydactyl" cats.

Glossary

animal shelter place where lost or unwanted animals are looked after

collar band worn around the neck

disease sickness

fur ball ball of fur in a cat's stomach. The cat has to vomit to get rid of a fur ball.

groom brush your cat's fur. Cats also groom themselves by using their rough tongues.

litter box box where a cat can go to the bathroom. The box is filled with special gravel called litter.

microchip tiny tag with a special number on it to help you find your cat if it gets lost

neutered when a male cat has surgery so that it cannot have any babies

spayed when a female cat has surgery so that it cannot have any babies

veterinarian specially trained animal doctor

More Books to Read

An older reader can help you with these books.

Backaby, Susan. *A Cat For You: Caring For Your Cat.* Minneapolis, MN: Picture Window Books, 2003.

Boyer Binns, Tristan. *Keeping Pets: Cats.* Chicago, ILL.: Heinemann Library, 2004.

Kim, Bryan. *How to Look After Your Pet: Kitten Care.* New York: Dorling Kindersley Publishing Inc., 2004.

Evans, Mark. *Kitten (ASPCA Pet Guides for Kids),* Minneapolis, MN: Turtleback Books, 2002.

Roca, Nuria and Rosa M. Curto. *Let's Take Care of Our New Cat.* New York: Barron's Educational Series, 2006.

Index

animal shelter 8

claws 5, 19

collar 28

fleas 9, 28

food 14, 15, 28

handling 12, 16

lifespan 26

litter box 11, 18

neutered 21

pet carrier 12

scratching post 19

spayed 21

training 16

whiskers 5